Table of Contents

When I Married Chris Thomas	1
At the Hotel	3
Customers Who Wanted Moonshine	4
The Saturday Evening I'm Talking About,	5
Monday Morning I Didn't Unlock the Doors.	7
Chris Talked to Someone out on a Plantation.	8
If You Were a Good Workman	9
I Had an Eye for Business.	11
Open Pit Barbecue	12
And I'd Make Bromley Stew	13
"What Are You Cooking?"	14
"Draw Day"	15
I Let the Men Gamble and Play Cards.	16
I'll Tell You How I Stopped with It.	17
The Day before My Husband Was Gonna Leave for St. Louis	19
Chris Left a Certain Amount with Me.	20
When Monday Morning Came	21
When He Come Back to See, I Said,	24
He Was Sorry.	25

Miss Ella's Kitchen Door	26
Butter in a Jar	28
My Husband Was in St. Louis	29
I Liked to Can.	30

A Note

Jerred Metz's Books

About the Poet

When I Married Chris Thomas

in 1911 we had money.
We owned a horse and buggy.
We bought a rooming house
a couple was selling
in Monticello, Georgia.
We named it the Thomas Hotel
after our name.

We honeymooned
at Indian Spring.

To get there we crossed a creek
on a wide platform, a ferry.
A man pulled on ropes
to get us across.
I was scared to death
because all along
there wasn't nothing
but water.
We reached the landing
and just drove the buggy off.

Indian Spring had steep long
wooden steps
leading down to it.

They claimed
 the water

was good for you.
You paid a dime
for the dipper.
The water tasted pretty good
and it smelled like rotten eggs.
Every time you'd dip
your dipper
you'd drink
your dipper dry.

At the Hotel

I ran the restaurant.
I kept ice in a
long ice box
with sliding doors.

The Saturday I'm talking about
I bought a load of
watermelons and cantaloupe
and put them in the ice box.
I made ice cream,
cakes and potato pie.
They were in the ice box
to sell. I put a big dishpan
full of fish and one of
stew meat in there.

That morning I got fifteen crates
of flavored soda water.
My husband's friend
delivered us moonshine.
I mixed alcohol
with half a bottle of Coca-Cola.
Two shelves up yonder
had the mixed soda.
The soda I didn't mix
I had in the ice box, too.

Customers Who Wanted Moonshine

would say,
"Give me a warm soda, Iola."
Regular soda was 15 cents,
mixed was fifty.
The law didn't know
I was doing it.

The Saturday Evening I'm Talking About,

Chris came in the kitchen.
>"Sweetheart, you been in here
>all day and night
>cooking and getting things ready.
>Go in and lay down for a while.
>I'll take over for you."

I took him at his word.
I went to bed.
He drank all the mixed soda
and fell dead asleep in the kitchen
with the door open.
Someone came in and took
everything I had in the ice box.
I had laid enough in there
to pay our mortgage
and buy everything I needed
after I sold what I had cooked.
When I saw what happened
I let Chris have it.
>"Chris, where is everything?"

>"What do you mean?"

>"Where is all the watermelons,
>soda water, my fish, stew meat,
>cakes and pies?"

>"Damned if I know."

I was so mad I didn't know what to do.

"Now you know the mortgage is due on Monday."

Monday Morning I Didn't Unlock the Doors.

10:30 I opened them.
Then everything people wanted,
I just give it to them for nothing.
They want a cigar,
I give it to them.
They want cigarettes, chewing
gum, tobacco, I give it to them.
Everyone that come in
I give them whatever they called for.
I didn't charge them nothing,
not a penny.

Chris Talked to Someone out on a Plantation.

The man, Mr. Leverett, said,

>"You come to the country for a year.
>I'll pay you forty dollars a month."

Chris asked me,

>"Will you come with me to the country?"

See, I was going with him anyhow.
I was crazy about him,
but he didn't know that.
I just said,

>"Maybe. I don't know."

When we got to the plantation
Chris said to me,

>"I told the boss that you didn't know
>nothing about farming
>or anything like that.
>I hired myself out, not you.
>I told him not to bother you
>no time about going to the fields."

So the boss didn't,
at least not then.

If You Were a Good Workman

At that time if you were a good workman you didn't get away like you thought. They said a year then they kept you saying you still owed them some money. I didn't let Chris buy no groceries or clothes or nothing on time. When he'd go to the store I'd give him money to buy what I wanted. Christmas came and the plantation owner was going to figure up everything to see what we owed and what we didn't owe.

> "Chris, take all these receipts with you
> and let the boss figure to see
> you don't owe anything."

The boss figured and said we
owe seventy-five dollars.

> "I don't owe anything!"

I asked Chris,

> "What about the receipts you carried?"

> "The boss said I overlooked some of them.
> I'm leaving here."

Chris had a sister and brother in St. Louis.

> "I'm not gonna stay. I'm going to St. Louis."

> "I'd hate for you to go.
> Something might happen to your
> people back here and you might
> have to come back. Then the
> boss will arrest you and
> say you left owing money."

So he stayed on a while longer.
All the next year he worked and worked.

In the meantime his uncle passed.
The boss wouldn't let him off
to go to the burial.
It made Chris mad and
I didn't like it either.

I Had an Eye for Business.

I was dressing hair down to the
country and I made good money.
I bought two hogs and my sow had nine pigs.
The men would go to town on Saturday.
One Saturday they'd go to get food.
The next Saturday—"draw day"—
they could draw money.
When it was "draw day"
I'd treat a pig for barbecue.

Open Pit Barbecue—

that was some good barbecue.

I had a pit dug deep in the ground,
iron rods across. When I got it like I wanted,
I put on oak and hickory.
I didn't cook with no pine.
I made a fire under and
let all the wood burn out
till it was coals.
Then I would lay
a whole hog
or calf
or a lamb
across on those iron rods.
Grease would drip down from that
hog and keep the fire burning.
Once in a while I'd turn the hog
and let it cook on the other side.
The drippings and smoke were underneath.
The hog would cook for
A long time and then
it would start browning.

You talk about something good!

And I'd Make Bromley Stew

out of the head.

I'd take it and
the liver and lights,

the heart and kidneys and ears
and everything like that,

boil it, then cut it
all up together.

Then I would mix up tomatoes,
red pepper, black pepper,

salt and vinegar.
I would hang a big pot

outside and make
a fire under it.

People would come along,
white people, too,

and smell the cooking,
smelling so good.

"What Are You Cooking?"

      "Bromley stew."

      "How you sell it?"

      "25 cents a bowl."

      "I'll take a bowl.
      And what else you cooking?"

      "I'm barbecuing a pig."

Sometimes they'd buy $3.00
worth of meat
right there. Sure, I had
a head for business
in those times.

Cooking them hogs up and holding
dances is where I got the money
to send my husband to St. Louis

"Draw Day"

On the afternoon of "draw day"
I'd send Chris to town for
apples, oranges, candy,
cigarettes, and cigars.

We'd have a big dance
that night at the house.
We had wonderful music
with guitars and fiddles.
You talk about dancing!
We did the kind of dance
where they call figures.
When a dance was over
the men would take their partners
and promenade on home to the
stand where all the food was laid.
The men would treat their partners.
I'd be right there selling barbecue.

I Let the Men Gamble and Play Cards.

They'd sit by and lose everything they had.
One man said,

> "Mr. Thomas, I never come to your house
> on account of your wife is good luck to you
> and I can't win a thing."

Chris won everything.
I'd sit right there by him.
I let the men gamble,
but I didn't like it.
I wanted Chris to get enough money
to get away from the plantation
as quick as he could
so I let him gamble.

I'll Tell You How I Stopped with It.

I call myself a Christian.

I had been going to church
since I was a little kid.

One Friday morning there
wasn't a cloud in the sky.

And after a while it come on
one big, spotted cloud

right over my house. It thundered
and there was lightning.

I was in the kitchen making
some cucumber pickle.

I had the pan on the stove.
The lightning come.

It split the ceiling joist
clean on down from one end

to the other right
over my kitchen stove

and knocked that pan of
pickles down on the floor

and not a drop of the
juice spilled out.

I was standing.
The lightning jumped right over me.

It struck right over my head
and it was awful hot.

I could feel a
stinging like sand.

The lightning struck clean
on out in the kitchen

right across from the kitchen
door and ended in the corner.

That was a warning.
I was doing wrong

and I stopped.
From then on I

didn't let no more gambling
go on in my house.

The Day before My Husband
Was Gonna Leave for St. Louis

was "draw day."

We fixed everything up.
We told the ladies and men
we were gonna have a party.

In those times nobody didn't
come to parties unless
they was invited.

We didn't invite any and everybody.
Only certain people were invited.
They came all dressed up
and dolled up.

Chris picked out a big red
hog with a short nose
to barbeque
and I picked out one
with a pretty curly tail.

That night we sold out
everything, made good money.

Chris Left a Certain Amount with Me.

I washed all his socks and pressed
all his shirts and pants.
I fixed his grip, had it all ready.
We had a friend who was going north
to St. Louis, too. They couldn't
just go to the depot
and get on the train.
They had a friend take their grips
to the depot, buy their tickets
and bring the tickets back.
When the time come to go
they went to the depot and
got on the train without
anybody seeing them.
He had to slip away.
You couldn't just leave.
You hired yourself out to
somebody for a certain amount
and when the time is out
they make like you owe them
even when you didn't
owe them anything.
It was almost slavery.

Chris left that Sunday.

> "I'm going away
> and I'll keep in touch."

When Monday Morning Came

Mr. Leverett came around.

> "Iola, where's Chris?"

> "I don't know, Mr. Leverett.
> He left home yesterday
> and he didn't come back."

I was pregnant.

> "I'm surprised at him.
> He was so crazy about his wife.
> He went away and left you like that?"

> "He certainly did."

I was just so calm, didn't know a thing.
Next morning Mr. Leverett come back.

> "Iola, Chris ain't come back yet?"

> "No, sir."

> "Well, I'm surprised."

> "Me, too. I just don't know what to think."

Mr. Leverett kept on,
kept that up for a week.

He saw Chris wasn't coming back.

"Well, Iola, what you gonna do?
You can come over to the house.
You could cook.
You're a damn good cook,

a nice, quiet, clean person.
Won't you come and move in the house
where the hands come to eat
and cook for them?"

"No, sir. You know when my husband
was here he didn't allow me in the kitchen
where all those men come eating and
cussing and fussing and fighting
over the food.
I wouldn't come
now just because
he's not here."

"Well, I tell you what I'll do.
I'll empty the kitchen
and I'll have the hands
to eat someplace else.

You can come and stay here
till this thing's over.

Then after your baby's born you can keep your baby and I'll have someone to tend to it while you work in the kitchen."

"I'll think about it, Mr. Leverett."

"You let me know in a couple of weeks."

When He Come Back to See, I Said,

"I have relatives over the hill there.
They don't want me to be by myself.
My uncle lives right across the street
and they want me to move in there.

I can't come and work for you."

He Was Sorry.

But you know what he did?
He tried to catch me
and make me stay.

> "Your husband come to town
> and bought sixty dollars worth of furniture."

> "I wonder where he put it.
> You see, I have three rooms
> of the nicest furniture you ever saw.
> He couldn't have done it.
> If you don't believe me
>
> go down to the hardware store
> and the dry goods store
> and the grocery
> and find out
>
> all what I bought
> and paid for."

> "Well, this gramophone,
> he did take this up."

> "No, I bought that, too,
> before me and Chris were married."

Miss Ella's Kitchen Door

After my mother died when I was a little kid a white lady raised me. She was crazy about me. She didn't want me to leave after she raised me from a little kid on up. She had built me a two room house. My house was right step out of Miss Ella's kitchen door into my door. I was married in that house. I was over at my uncle's when she said,

> "Tell Iola to come down."

She had cows and a churn.

> "Have Iola come down and churn
> for me and take up the butter."

She was all in tears when I got there.

> "Iola, you didn't marry who
> I wanted you to marry.
> That boy's family have a big farm
> and their own home and stock."

> "Miss Ella, I didn't know that boy
> you wanted me to marry.
>
> He would have made you a good husband.
> See what happened?
> You followed your fancy
> and now your husband's gone.

You married Chris Thomas.
I told you he would give you a
house full of children
then go off

and leave you.
And that's just
what he did.
You're just unlucky."

"Yes, ma'am, he sure did."

And I looked so pitiful.

Butter in a Jar

Miss Ella thought he had left me
like the other people thought.
I went down and churned for her.
When I got through I took up the butter
and put up the milk and, like a mother
would do, when I got ready to go home,
she put a great big chunk of butter in a jar
and filled it the rest of the way with milk.

> "Iola, if you ever want to come back
> to your own house
> it will always be here for you.
> And another thing:
> you can't, if Chris sends for you,
> get so far
> that my money can't reach you."

Then she hugged me and kissed me, and
with tears in her eyes, seeming to know
what the truth of it was, sent me on my way.

My Husband Was in St. Louis

All this time my husband was
in St. Louis where his
people were. I knew
where he was all the time.
But you had to surprise the boss.
Chris' brother got him a job at
the terminal roundhouse.
He sent me thirty dollars
by my sister in-law, not to me,
now. He had to send it to someone
he could trust and she brought
it to me. He wrote a note:
"The next time I send you money
I want you to come away from there.
Don't pack up anything.
Just take your bedding and clothing
and some of your cooking things,
 all you can put in a trunk,
and bring it on. And just leave the house."

I Liked to Can.

I had every kind of fruit.
I had a food safe
and I couldn't bear to leave
all that fruit in there.
My sister and my brother
lived in the same town with me.

> "I'm going.
> This fruit and everything in here,
> you divide it up.
> Take all you want.
> It belongs to you."

And that's the way it ended up.
The next thing I knew,
I was in St. Louis.

A Note

I met Iola Buckner in 1978 at the Darst-Webbe Senior Citizen Apartments in St. Louis, Missouri. I had been hired to teach ten sessions of creative writing. After the third week it became clear that the three folks who showed up each time were masterful at telling about events from their lives. Instead of teaching them, we engaged in a two and a half year project of weekly Friday hour-long meetings that produced the work of oral literature—*Drinking the Dipper Dry: Nine Plain-Spoken Lives*.

Iola's story of her first marriage into a life of prosperity and the change the loss of the hotel and restaurant wrought in the Thomas' life stayed with me.

Both its power and its poetic quality compelled me to slow up the telling, add the elements of poetry—line break and stanza—of the two years in her life, present it as narrative poems.

Jerred Metz

Jerred Metz's Books

Poetry

Brains, 25 Cents: Drive In

Angels in the House

The Temperate Voluptuary

*Three Legs Up, Cold as Stone;
Six Legs Down, Blood and Bone*

Speak Like Rain

Prose

The Angel of Mons: A World War I Legend

The Last Eleven Days of Earl Durand

Halley's Comet, 1910: Fire in the Sky

Drinking the Dipper Dry: Nine Plain-Spoken Lives